Games of
Strength and Skill

THE MARSHALL CAVENDISH
ILLUSTRATED GUIDE TO

GAMES
CHILDREN
PLAY
AROUND THE WORLD

Games of
Strength and Skill

Ruth Oakley
Illustrated by Steve Lucas

Marshall Cavendish
New York · London · Toronto · Sydney

Library Edition 1989

© Marshall Cavendish Limited 1989
© DPM Services Limited 1989

Published by Marshall Cavendish Corporation
　　　　　　　147 West Merrick Road
　　　　　　　Freeport
　　　　　　　Long Island
　　　　　　　N.Y. 11520

Produced by DPM Services Limited
Designed by Graham Beehag

Library of Congress Cataloging-in-Publication Data

Oakley, Ruth,
　　Games of strength and skill/written by Ruth Oakley: Illustrated
by Steve Lucas.
　　　　p.　　cm. − (Games children play).
　　Includes index.
　　Summary: Offers instructions for a selection of games that test a
variety of skills and strengths.
　　ISBN 1-85435-084-6:
　　1. Games−Juvenile literature. [1. Games.] I. Lucas, Steve,
[1]. II. Title. III. Series: Oakley, Ruth. Games children play.
GV1203.026 1989
793.8−dc19　　　　　　　　　　　　　　　　　　　　88-28712
　　　　　　　　　　　　　　　　　　　　　　　　　　　CIP
　　　　　　　　　　　　　　　　　　　　　　　　　　　AC

ISBN 1-85435-076-5 (set):

Printed and bound in Italy by L.E.G.O. SpA, Vicenza

Contents

If you watch a kitten or puppy playing, you can see that the games it plays are actually improving the skills it will need for survival in its adult life. The kitten jumps and turns and chases. It paws and and tries to catch anything fluttering at eye level. It crawls and stalks the piece of paper tied on a string which is pulled in front of it. It is learning how to hunt.

Similarly, some of the traditional activities of children improve their physical and mental skills. Most of us enjoy a challenge and are prepared to keep trying until we have mastered a particular skill.

Children today will practice for hours until they can perform stunts on their B.M.X. bicycles in much the same way as the children around the world have always persevered to perfect their skills, although most of their equipment was simple and cheap.

Tops are not as popular today as they were in the past, but for thousands of years, they amused children from Europe to Asia and the Americas. In Japan, they are called **koma**, the name of the part of Korea where the Japanese first saw them in the eighth century. They can be made from wood, bamboo, shell, or metal. Some have holes cut in them so that they make a humming sound when spun. **Beigoma** were originally

B.M.X. bikes such as this one are good for stunts.

6

made by filling a spiral seashell with sand and lead and spun with a whipcord. Wooden tops are still made in many places, including England and Bangladesh.

The people of the Dominican Republic call tops **Moteca**, and they play a game with spinning tops and buttons. A circle is drawn on the ground, and inside it are placed buttons resting on flat stones. The players are not allowed inside this circle. Each player in turn spins her top, scoops it into her hand,

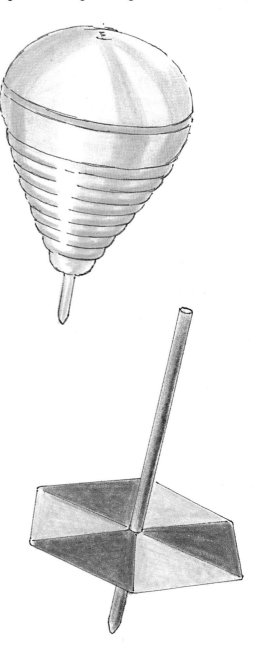

and keeping it spinning, she throws it into the circle to try to knock a button off a stone and out of the circle. If she succeeds, she keeps the button and has another turn. If the button is not knocked out of the circle, it is replaced on the stone and the next player has a turn.

Playing Moteca.

8

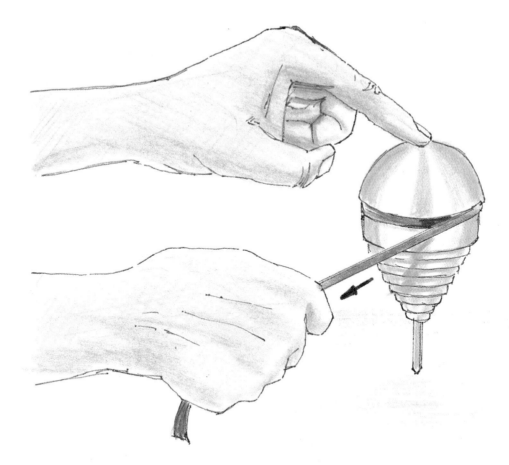

Spinning a top with a leather thong.

To spin a top, you need a leather thong about half a yard long. Some tops are shaped like a mushroom; you wind the thong around their shanks. Peg tops are pear-shaped; on them, you wind the thong around the body. The difficult part is to get the top started!

One way is to hold the top in one hand between your thumb and index finger. Jerk the string off quickly with the other hand, and let the top fall to the ground where it will spin if you have done it properly. To spin a peg top which has a metal peg or point at its base, steady it in a slight depression in the ground by resting one finger on the head of the top, and then quickly pull your thong away.

You will have to persevere. Once your top is spinning, you can whip it to keep it going. Skillful players can make their tops jump.

The **yo-yo** is another simple-looking toy which needs practice before you can get much fun out of it. Yo-yos are readily available and inexpensive to buy. As with so many of the toys and games described in these books, the Greeks and Romans played with yo-yos, although they may have first been made in the Philippines long before.

To make a yo-yo work, wind the string around it, hold it in the palm of your hand, and let it drop. By gently rocking your hand, you can make the yo-yo continue to return to your hand many times. You can make it swing and jump as well when you have really got the knack.

An even simpler game which is also very old and very widespread is rolling **hoops**. Existing illustrations show ancient Greeks rolling hoops. Roman children enjoyed them as well and attached bells to them so that they jingled as they were bowled along. Hoops can be made from wood, metal, or, as they usually are today, plastic.

Most hoop games are based on rolling them, either with the palm of the hand or with a stick.

You can also skip with a hoop if you get one big enough, and they can be used with great effect in gymnastic displays.

In the 1950s, there was a craze for using hoops as hula hoops. Put the hoop over your head, and hold it at your waist. Give it a spin to start it off, and then gyrate your hips to keep the hoop spinning and stop if from dropping down your legs.

You can have races with hoops, either individually or in teams as a relay. To have a relay, divide into equal teams with a hoop for each team. You need a starting line and a finish line drawn on the ground. On the starting signal, the first player from each team drives his hoop up to the finishing line and

back again and passes the hoop to the next player in his team.

If the hoop falls to the ground at any stage, that player has to return to the starting line and begin again. The first team with all its players successfully completing the course is the winning team. You might like to make the game more difficult by putting obstacles such as stones or cartons along the course to maneuver through.

Another game which can be turned into a relay race is **Leapfrog**. To play, one person makes "a back" by bending over and holding his knees with his hands. He can either bend his knees or keep his legs straight, depending on how good at jumping the other player is. The jumper runs up, puts his hands on the "back," and jumps over from the back to the front or sideways.

To have a race, choose teams of equal numbers — about six

each is a good number. Line up in teams, one behind the other, with a gap of about one and a half yards between each player and a space of about four yards in front of the first player. All except the last member of each team make "backs."

On the starting signal, the last player on each team leap-frogs over all the other members of his team and makes a "back" in front of the first player. Then, the player who is now at the back does the same thing, and so on, until all the players have returned to their original positions. If you do not have enough room, the teams will have to shunt back between each turn. The team which is first to complete all the jumps wins.

Sliding is fun, but should be played somewhere safe. The children in the photograph are enjoying sliding down a slope on a plastic sheet made slippery with water. An old tray in the snow has the same effect. Sand dunes are good for slides, and in Nigeria, there are great rocks where one tribe used to have sliding ceremonies.

Sliding on a wet plastic sheet.

The Eskimos play a game of skill called **Alaskan Aratamiaqutat**, or Alaskan Highkick.

A target is suspended about eighteen inches from the ground. The Eskimos use a piece of fur hanging from a stick, but you could use any old cloth or a paper plate on a string. Sit on the floor and grasp one of your feet with the opposite hand. Use your other hand and foot to balance, and then try to kick the target with your free foot. As you improve your aim, raise the target.

Another Eskimo game is **Ajagaak**, or Ajaraq. The Eskimos make the equipment they need from a seal bone with a hole bored in it. This is attached with string to a wooden point. The aim of the game is to get the wooden point in the bone as you throw the bone in the air, similar to the Elizabethan game of Cup and Ball, which is still made and played in England and India.

"Ken" is the Japanese word for fist and also means games played with the fist. These games were probably brought to Japan from China in the seventeenth century. One of them is **Kazuken** (numbered fist). Players face each other, and on a signal, they each extend any number of fingers, at the same time shouting out their guess as to how many fingers their opponent will show.

The Romans called this game **Micare**, and the Italians say **Uno, Cinque, Sette.**

Another "ken" game is **Janken**, which is the Japanese version of a game played by children in many European countries, especially Italy. It is a hand game for a group of children and needs no equipment.

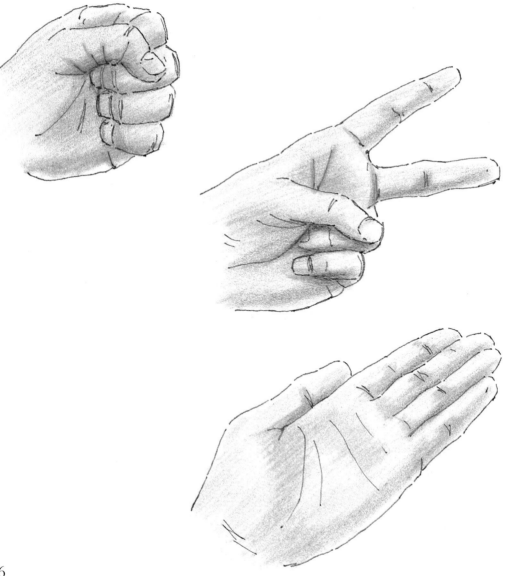

Stone sharpens scissors.

First, choose a "changer," who is the player who sets the challenge for the rest.

You use your hand to represent stone, paper, and scissors. Stone is a closed fist. Scissors is two fingers extended. Paper is the hand held flat with the palm turned up.

The changer stands in front of the group with his hand as a fist and moves it up and down three times from the elbow saying, "Jan, ken, pon." At the last "Jan, ken, pon," the changer quickly makes either stone, paper, or scissors.

If he makes stone, the other players must make paper because paper covers stone. Similarly, scissors cut paper and stone sharpens scissors. The person who twice makes the correct sign the quickest becomes the next changer.

If you have a large group, you might need a referee to see who is quickest.

The Chinese have a game using five fingers, which is played in the same way as Janken.

The thumb represents the sun, the index finger is clouds, the middle finger is wind, the ring finger is smoke, and the little finger is eyes.

The order of precedence is that the sun is hidden by clouds; clouds are swept away by wind; wind chases smoke; smoke gets in the eyes. If the changer shows the little finger for eyes, the players must rub their eyes to wipe away the tears caused by the smoke.

You could make up your own games like these, perhaps using finger puppets or changes based on the different characteristics of various animals.

Playing Janken in a group.

Simon Says, or O'Grady Says, is a game for a group of children of any age from about five years old. All you need is some space, indoors or out. "Simon" stands facing the rest of the players, who arrange themselves so that they can hear and see him clearly. It is a good idea to have a referee if there are a

lot of players, or if you are playing for a prize at a party, but normally Simon decides who is out.

Simon does an action such as standing on one leg and says, "Simon says, stand on one leg," and everyone copies the action. Simon continues with any actions he can think of, but if he just says, "Do this," the others must NOT copy him. Anyone who does is out. If Simon calls out his instructions quickly, one after the other, he will soon get some people out. The last player in is the winner and becomes the new Simon. Some people play that Simon can say one action but do another to trip people up. The players have to do what Simon says, not what he does.

Another game which is often played at parties is **Kim's Game**. A selection of fairly small, but ordinary and everyday, objects are put on a tray. You need about twenty objects, such as a screw, a key, a coin, a piece of string, a spoon, a die, a scarf, a pin, a match, a small toy, a piece of paper, a pencil, and so on.

The tray is placed so that each of the players can see clearly what is on it. They then have a set period of time — say half a minute or a minute — to try to remember all the objects without writing anything down. Then the tray is removed, and the players are given three or four minutes to write down as many of the objects as they can remember. The winner is the one who remembers the most correctly. Some people will invariably write down things which were not even on the tray.

Chuke is played by some Indians in South America, and games very much like it are played by many North American Indians as well. In some ways, it is rather like the board games of Pachisi and Ludo. It is also similar to Nyout, which is played in Korea.

A typical collection of household items chosen for Kim's Game.

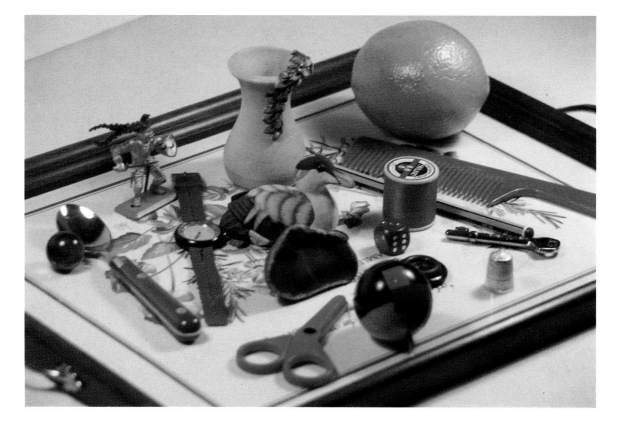

Traditionally, Chuke is played in March. The players carve their own wooden blocks for the game, which are thrown like dice to determine what moves are made. The blocks are rectangular and flat on one side and curved on the other, and the Indians take pride in decorating them. Each player has four blocks. They score as follows:

4 curved or 4 flat sides up — move 5 squares
3 curved and 1 flat sides up — move 4 squares
2 curved and 2 flat sides up — move 3 squares
1 curved and 3 flat sides up — move 2 squares

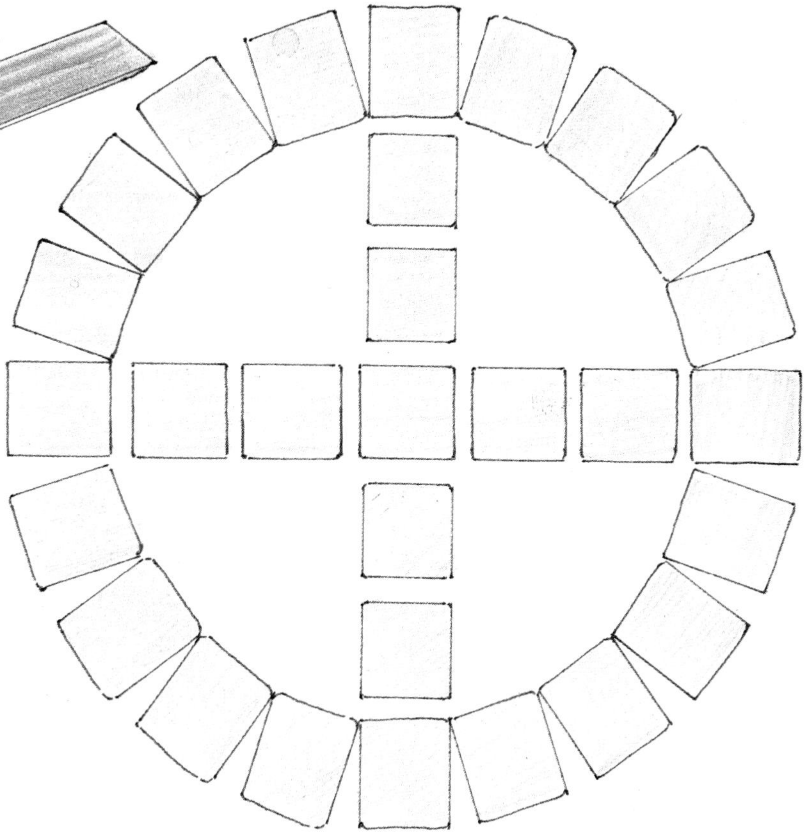

Each player has four men, which are usually pebbles.

The game is played on a board drawn on the ground, consisting of a circle of twenty squares, with another nine squares dividing the circle into quarters (see diagram). The men move around the board in a counter-clockwise direction according to the throws of the blocks. The aim of the game is to get all the men around the circle and back to the square at the top. Two, three, or four people may play. A game with four players is played with two pairs; each pair has four men. A move may be taken with one man or divided among two or more men. Only one man may occupy a square at a time, and only one man can be passed by in any one move.

If a player lands on one of the squares at the junction with the quarter lines, he is allowed to move to the center square, and he has another turn.

The game is a combination of luck and skill, because you have to decide which is the best route to take — around the circle or across it — because the opposition may block your path.

Le Herradura, or Horseshoe Quoits, was played by the Spaniards and the Incas of Peru and spread to the ranches of the United States and Australia. Although horseshoes were traditionally used, you can play a similar game with any heavy rings.

Two stakes are driven into the ground, and players take turns to try to throw horseshoes over them. Agree your own line from which to throw and a system of scoring. You will need scores for getting the ring right over the peg, hitting the peg, or being the nearest to it.

Traveling country fairs in England usually have **Hoopla stalls** where players try to throw light rubber rings over prizes on the stall. You win only if the ring falls right over the prize onto the table!

Bean curd, or tofu, a soft "cheese" made from soybean milk, is a staple ingredient in China and other Oriental countries. The cheese is made on big trays and cut into squares or triangles. Children in Hong Kong play a game called **Cut the Bean Curd**. The game is for five players. Four of the players stand on the four corners of a square drawn on the ground and the fifth is the "caller," who stands in the middle and tells the others what to do.

"Cut the bean curd crosswise." Players opposite each other change places diagonally.

"Cut the bean curd straight." Players change places by moving along the edges of the square.

"Carry the water across the river." Opposite players change places, hopping on the right foot while pretending to carry a heavy pail.

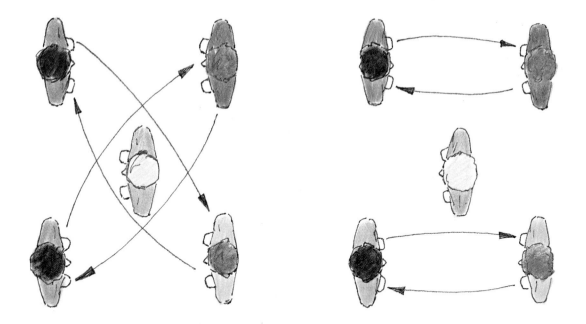

This diagram
shows the
movements for *Cut
the Bean Curd*.

"Carry your shoe to the shoemaker." As before, but hopping on the left foot, pretending to carry a shoe.

"Move a tree." All the players stand their ground, and the caller tries to drag one of them into the middle to be the new caller.

To make the game fast, the caller has to call out the commands quickly to get people confused.

Another fast game with commands you have to listen to and learn is **All the Fish in the Sea**. Any number can play, indoors or out. Between fifteen and forty players of any age works best.

The game begins with all the players except one, the caller, sitting on the ground in a circle. The caller goes around the circle, giving each person in turn the name of a kind of fish: "Herring, cod, flounder, herring, cod flounder, etc." You need about eight to ten of each fish, so if there are 24 players, you'll need three different kinds, etc.

The commands are:

"Flounder (or any of the other fish) are swimming." All the flounders jump up and run around the outside of the circle and back to their places and sit down.

"All the fish in the sea are swimming." Everyone jumps up, runs around the circle, and sits down in their places.

"Tide's turning." This is called while players are already

running; they have to turn around and run in the opposite direction. The caller can call this as often as she likes.

Each time, the last person back to her place is out and has to stand up in her place. The last person sitting is the winner and becomes the new caller.

Man Overboard also has a nautical theme. You can play with two or more teams or individually. You need a caller and perhaps some judges if a lot of children are playing. The game begins with everyone sitting down, in lines if you are playing with teams.

The commands and actions are:

"All the deck." Everyone jumps up.

"Scrub the decks." Pretend to scrub the decks kneeling down.

"Bombs overhead." Kneel down with hands over head.

"Captain's coming." Jump up, stand to attention, and salute.

"Man overboard." Run and touch the nearest wall, run back to place, and sit down.

"Climb the rigging." Stand up and pretend to climb up the sail ropes.

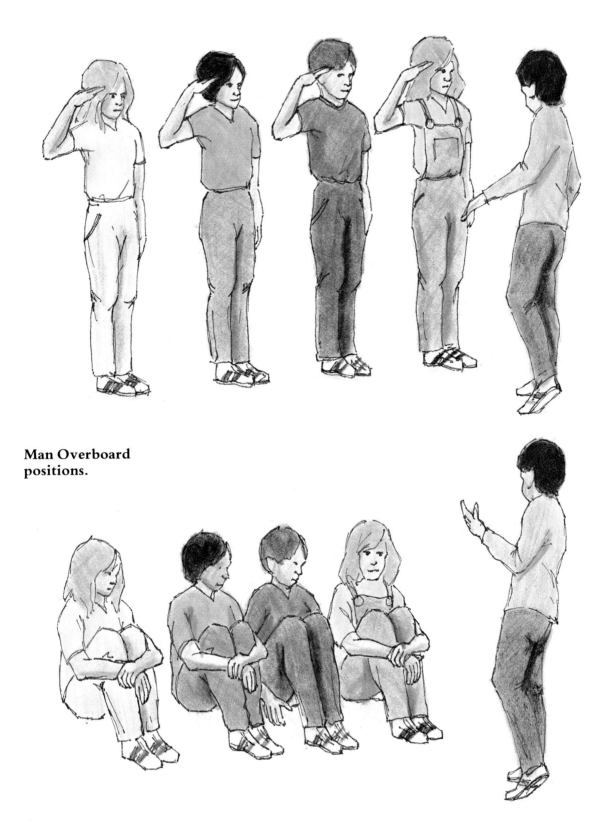

Man Overboard positions.

The slowest person to react each time is out, and the winning team is the last one to have any members still in it.

A team game from Nigeria is a war canoe contest. Each team needs between four and eight children and a pole about two yards long — a broomstick or a thick bamboo cane will do. As many teams as you like may take part in the contest. Unless you have a lot of space and equipment, it is easier if they race two teams at a time, with the winning teams racing against each other until there is one winning team left.

The idea of the game is to pretend that the team is rowing a war canoe down the river, avoiding the rocks or mud banks or hungry crocodiles!

A start and finish line are marked on the ground about 15 yards apart; the space between them is the river. Obstacles such as stones or chairs or cartons are placed in the "river" to represent natural hazards and to make a winding course like a river.

The teams stand holding the stick between their legs and with their backs to the river, except for the steersman for each team, who faces the river.

On the starting signal, the crews run backwards trying to follow the directions of the steersmen and make their way around the obstacles to the finishing line as quickly as possible.

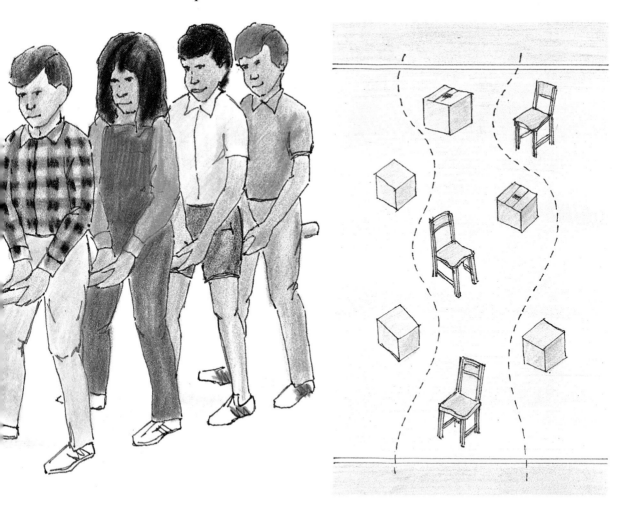

Chenille–assis is a team game from Belgium which imitates the movement of a caterpillar. You can have as many teams as you like or have room for, but you need at least five people in each team. Each team should be positioned about four yards apart, and there should be about ten yards between the starting and the finish lines.

The game begins with the teams sitting down in rows, with one player behind another. The players have their legs bent

and their feet flat on the floor. Each child sits between the feet of the player behind him and holds that player's ankles.

To move, each member of the team shifts his weight from his feet to his seat, still keeping hold of the ankles of the person behind. The first team to get all its members across the finishing line is the winner.

Another game which imitates the movement of an animal is the **Kangaroo Hop Race** from Australia. It can be played either as an individual race or a relay event.

To play, make yourself look like a kangaroo by holding

your arms up to your chest with your fingers pointing down and your elbows tucked in. Then, keeping your legs together and bent at the knees, make big kangaroo hops as quickly as you can along the track from the start to the finish line.

If it is a relay race, the teams line up behind each other at the starting line. On the starting signal, the first member of each team kangaroo–hops to the finish line and back again, and then tags the next member of his team. The first team whose members all complete the course wins the race.

English children play the same game, but as **Bunny Hops**. Start by crouching with your hands and feet on the ground and your knees bent so that your feet are touching your hands. Then, move your hands forward and jump your feet forward to meet them again. Repeat these movements so that you jump along the track.

In Puerto Rico, children play a game which is based on the fights which barnyard roosters have. It is a game for two children; each needs a stick about a yard long.

Bunny hops.

A circle about one and a half yards in diameter is drawn in the ground, and the two "roosters" squat inside it with their sticks tucked under their knees and their arms clasped around their legs.

The object of the game is to try to knock the other player off balance. The players must stay within the circle and must keep their arms around their knees so their sticks do not fall down.

Mancala is a game for which you have to learn to think ahead and to count carefully. Like Chess and Checkers, it is a game of strategy for two players, but it is played on a different kind of board. It is a game which is very old and widely played. Versions can be found throughout Africa, in parts of Asia, and in the Caribbean.

West African girls playing Mancala.

You can play it outside by making shallow holes in soft ground or sand and using stones or shells; or you can play indoors using a carved wooden board like the one in the picture, or make your own board and draw the circles on it.

Whichever kind of board you choose, you need twelve identical holes arranged in two rows of six, with two larger holes, one at each end. You also need forty-eight small stones, shells, or buttons; the game begins with four stones in each of the twelve smaller holes. The board is placed lengthwise between the two players, and the row of six holes nearest each player is his row.

To begin the game, one player takes all four stones out of any of his six holes. He distributes them one at a time in successive holes, moving around the board counterclockwise, but not using the two large holes at the end. Then the other player does the same, taking all the stones out of one of the holes on his side of the board.

The aim of the game is to capture as many stones as possible and place them in your trap, which is the largest hole at the end on your right.

To capture stones, place the last stone of your turn in a hole which has two or three stones in it, including the one you have just put in it. You then capture the other stones and put them in your trap. Now look at the hole before the one you have just emptied. If it contains two or three stones, you capture those as well. You keep going backwards and capturing until you reach a hole which has fewer than two, or more than three, stones in it. Then, it is the other player's turn.

You will find as you play that you sometimes get many stones in one hole. If there are more than twelve stones in one hole, skip that hole when you distribute your stones around the board.

You must always leave some stones in your opponent's holes, or he can capture all yours and end the game. If you reach a stage where neither of you can make any more captures, you each pick up the stones remaining in your holes. Put them in your traps, and count up to see who has the most. The player with the most stones in total is the winner.

Congklak is a very similar game played in Indonesia. In the Philippines, **Sunka** is played in much the same way, but there are seven holes in a row which represent huts, and the holes at the ends are called manors. The game begins with seven shells in each hut, and some of the rules are slightly different.

Moves in Mancala.

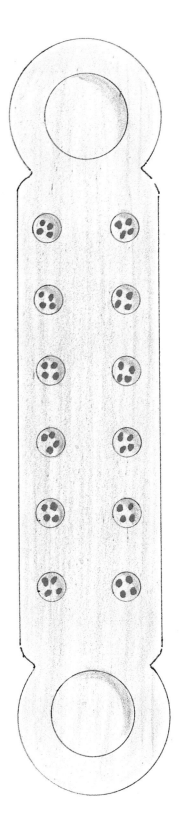
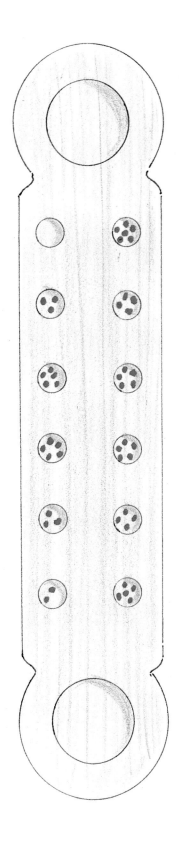

Most families have a set of **dominoes**, which are rectangles made of two equal squares side by side. They can be made of wood, plastic, bone, ivory, or cardboard. Sets are made for young children with pictures which they learn to match, but traditional dominoes are made with patterns of dots. The

lowest value "tile" (the name for a single domino) has no dots and is called a "double blank." A "double" is a tile which has the same number of dots on each of its halves. The next tile has one blank and one dot. Then comes one blank and two dots, and so on, until you reach "double six," which makes a

**Laying out your
tiles to play.**

**The basic set of
dominoes.**

set of twenty-eight tiles, as shown in the diagram.

You can get larger sets which go to "Double Nine" or "Double Twelve."

The simplest game is to lay all the tiles face down on the table. Each player draws five tiles, or seven if only two people are playing. Do not let the other players see your hand; either hold your tiles in your hand or stand them up on their edges with the dots facing you.

Take turns laying down a tile so that the number of dots matches the number of dots on one of the end tiles. The player

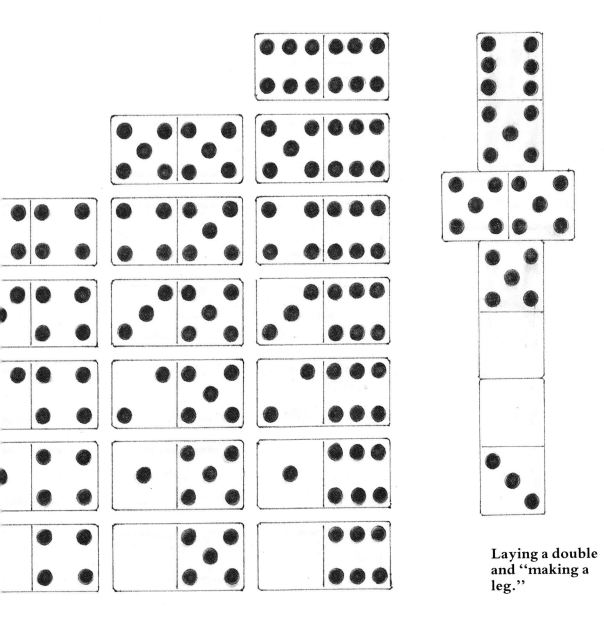

**Laying a double
and "making a
leg."**

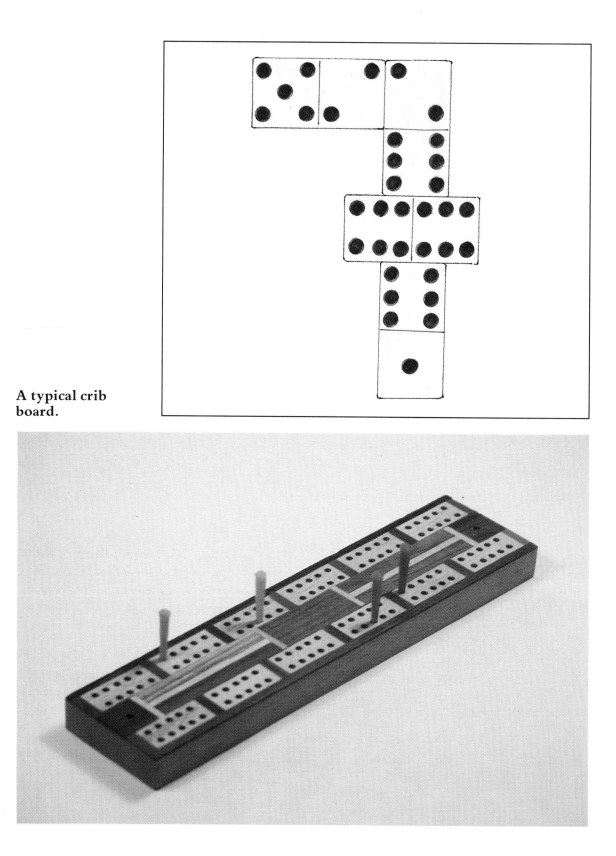

A typical crib
board.

with the highest double plays first. If you play a double, lay it at a right angle to the previous tile (see diagram). If you run out of space on the playing surface, turn a corner or "make a leg."

If you cannot go, rap your knuckle on the table. The first player to play all her tiles is the winner. Her score is the total of the number of dots on the tiles which the other players have not been able to play. If everyone has to knock, and no one can go out, the player with the least number of dots is the winner and scores the other players' dots, minus his own. Set a total which will be the winning score for the whole game, or you can use a special board with holes and pegs to move as counters. The first player to reach the end is the overall winner.

If there are four players, play as partners if you wish.

When there are dominoes left after the players have taken their agreed number, the spare tiles are left in the middle of the table, face down. This is called the "stock", the "woodpile," or the "boneyard." The last name comes from the days when dominoes were made of bone and ivory. You can decide what to do about them, but you must all agree before you begin to play. Either each player, when he cannot play any of his own tiles, may take one from the boneyard until the boneyard is empty, or until two tiles are left in the boneyard which must stay there. Another way to play is that all the tiles in the boneyard must stay there. This makes it impossible to know which number dominoes the other players are holding.

Variations on this game are to play Threes, Fives, or Fives and Threes. To play Threes, score by placing your tiles so that the spots at each end of the chain add up to a multiple of three. If you have a four at one end and a five at the other, the sum of dots is nine. This would score three because three threes are nine. You still have to match the number of dots on the halves of the tiles which touch each other.

Fives is played in the same way, except that you score for making multiples of five. For Fives and Threes, you can score either multiples of three or of five or of both. If someone makes a total of fifteen, that scores eight points: three for the fives and five for the threes. You must be careful about laying a double six, because that makes it easy for your opponent to make fifteen.

There are many other games you can play with dominoes, and the list of books at the back of this volume will help you find some of them if you are interested. Perhaps you can make up some new ones of your own and increase the variety of the games children play that you can pass on to others.

Glossary

characteristics Ways of acting which are usual for a particular person or animal.

circumference The outer edge of a circle.

counterclockwise Going around in the opposite direction to the way which the hands go around a clock.

diameter A line drawn across a circle from one point on the circumference to another which passes through the center of the circle.

Elizabethan The name given to the period of time during the reign of Queen Elizabeth I of England (1558-1603).

gyrate Revolve, twist in a circular movement.

hazard Danger.

knack Being able to do something which needs skill.

nautical To do with the sea and sailors.

precedence Power, importance.

rectangular Shaped like an oblong or rectangle.

shank The straight part of a top (like a leg).

stalk Move very quietly without being noticed when hunting.

strategy Planning ahead.

successive One after another.

thong Narrow strip of leather.

Index of Countries

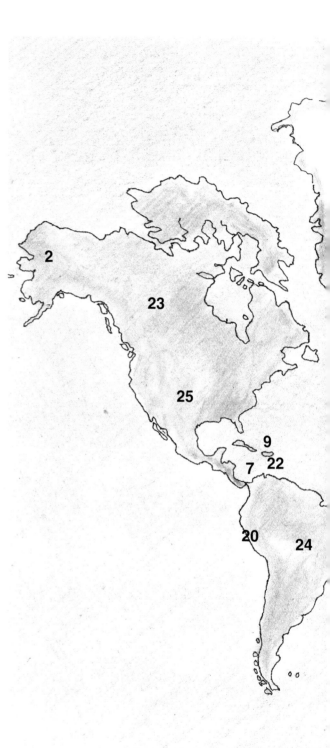

10   6   11

16   12

8

18   17

3

5

13

14

21

19   1

15

4

47

Index